Starting
a Business

The Lessons Learned Series

Wondering how the most accomplished leaders from around the globe have tackled their toughest challenges? Now you can find out—with Lessons Learned. Concise and engaging, each volume in this new series offers twelve to fourteen insightful essays by top leaders in business, the public sector, and academia on the most pressing issues they've faced.

A crucial resource for today's busy executive, Lessons Learned gives you instant access to the wisdom and expertise of the world's most talented leaders.

Other books in the series:

Leading by Example
Managing Change
Managing Your Career
Managing Conflict

LESSONS LEARNED

Starting
a Business

LES50NS
Boston, Massachusetts

Printed in the United States of America
11 10 09 08 07   5 4 3 2 1

Library of Congress Cataloging-in-Publication Data

Starting a business.
    p. cm. — (Lessons learned : straight talk from the world's top business leaders)
  ISBN 978-1-4221-2290-7
  1. New business enterprises. 2. Entrepreneurship—Anecdotes. 3. Entrepreneurship—Biography. 4. Businesspeople—Interviews. I. Fifty Lessons (Firm) II. Harvard Business School. Press.
  HD62.5.S7377 2007
  658.1'1—dc22

                                    2007037484

⊰ A NOTE FROM THE ⊱ PUBLISHER

In partnership with Fifty Lessons, a leading provider of digital media content,
Harvard Business School Press is pleased to
announce the launch of Lessons Learned,
a new book series that showcases the trusted
voices of the world's most experienced
leaders. Through the power of personal
storytelling, each book in this series pre-
sents the accumulated wisdom of some of
the world's best-known experts and offers
insights into how these individuals think,
approach new challenges, and use hard-won
lessons from experience to shape their leadership philosophies. Organized thematically
according to the topics at the top of managers' agendas—leadership, change management, entrepreneurship, innovation, and
strategy, to name a few—each book draws
from Fifty Lessons' extensive video library
of interviews with CEOs and other thought

A Note from the Publisher

leaders. Here, the world's leading senior executives, academics, and business thinkers speak directly and candidly about their triumphs and defeats. Taken together, these powerful stories offer the advice you'll need to take on tomorrow's challenges.

We invite you to join the conversation now. You'll find both new ways of looking at the world, and the tried-and-true advice you need to illuminate the path forward.

⤜⧏ CONTENTS ⧐⤏

Contents

Starting
a Business

——— ◆◆◆ ———

The Early Entrepreneurial Years

——— ◆◆◆ ———

Michael Dell

Founder, CEO, and Chairman, Dell, Inc.

I WAS A resourceful kid. I started with baseball cards, and then moved into stamps and gold and silver, and then into the stock market. The first job I got when I could actually drive—this was five or six jobs into my work experience—was working for the *Houston Post* newspaper. My job was to call

Starting a Business

people on the telephone and convince them to buy the newspaper. The first partial month I worked there, I figured out that when people wanted to buy the newspaper, either they were moving into a new house or apartment, or they'd just gotten married.

The way to find people who'd just gotten married was to go to the county courthouse. They have the applications for marriage licenses, which are a matter of public record in the state of Texas. And there is a place on the application form where you could request the license be sent. So that turned out to be a really good place to find people to whom I could send an offer to get the newspaper. The other thing I found was that you could actually get lists of people who had applied for and received mortgages. And that was another great list of people. My first full month at the paper, I was the top salesperson of newspapers, and I had a great time. This was a summer job. I started hiring my friends and sending them out to all the surrounding counties to collect all these lists of people who had applied for marriage licenses and just had a blast. I was sixteen years old. I saved my money and bought a new BMW.

When I was in my senior year in high school, we had a project in our government/economics class, which was to fill out our tax return. My teacher was really upset with me, because she thought I'd made a mistake because I'd made more than she did.

You have to experiment and look for new ways of doing things. Be resourceful. I learned an early lesson in the value of getting a direct contact with the customer—not doing it in a random way, but doing it in a very targeted way. I've always believed in looking at the problem in a different way and being resourceful.

At the beginning of the development of the PC, or what we know as the PC today, there were all sorts of dedicated computer stores that were selling PCs. And as a customer, I observed that it took a long time for the technology to actually get through the manufacturers, through the stores, and then to the customer. And it had an incredible cost by the time it got all the way through this long, complicated process. The people who were selling the products in the stores were just jumping onto a fad. They said, "Computers are the new thing in the eighties. Let's open a computer store." And there was a franchise model, so there were a lot of these stores popping up. As a customer, I was frustrated. It cost too much, took too long. The people in the store didn't know anything about it.

I knew there had to be a better way to do this. So I started taking apart more than a few computers, to understand what was inside them. I started by selling upgrade kits for computers, the memory, and the hard disk drives. At the time the PC didn't have a hard disk drive. So I would buy hard disk drives and controller cards. I'd make cables. I'd write software essentially to create a PC. That was really the origin of the company—in my dorm room. And it grew from there.

Within about a year we started to make our PCs, which it turns out wasn't that hard to do because all the components didn't come from the guys who were making the

Starting a Business

PCs; they came from the microprocessor company, the disk drive company, and the power supply company. This belief—that by working directly with customers we could get them the technology faster, provide a better level of service, and provide better value— was the basis of the business. The company grew about 80 percent per year for eight years in a row. We screwed up all kinds of things. But the fundamental business system was quite powerful and delivered lots of value to our customers.

We screwed up a lot of things, but the one thing that we really got right was this core business model, and it masked any other mistakes that we made. And we learned pretty quickly. We'd try something, and if it didn't work, we'd go do something else. You know, at my high school they didn't really teach us a whole lot about how to run a big computer company, so I was making it up as I was going along.

I've always been curious, and my curiosity has been rewarded, so I continue to be curious. I look for new ideas, new approaches. I don't really accept the status quo. I don't tend to be satisfied with the way things are. It's just in the wiring.

TAKEAWAYS

⊱ To succeed, entrepreneurs must experiment, be resourceful, and attack every situation in a very targeted way.

⊱ The importance of direct contact with customers cannot be underestimated. Their needs will be the basis of your business.

⊱ Along the way, recognize that you will "screw up." When mistakes are made, be prepared to try something else.

⊱ Don't accept the status quo. Curiosity will often lead to new ideas and new approaches.

Be Clear What the Aim Is

Sir Gerry Robinson

Former Chairman,
Allied Domecq

IT'S NEARLY IMPOSSIBLE to get somewhere if you're not clear where you're trying to go. It sounds so obvious, yet I have found over and over again, when I've looked at companies that are in trouble, that one of the key things that's missing is clarity about what they're trying to do.

Starting a Business

What is success? What is going to be the big tick in the box in three years' time, or in five years' time? That lack of clarity about where you're going creates an enormous number of problems and it's so simple and so straightforward, yet any number of times it doesn't happen.

For me, a very personal example is when I first arrived at Granada; it was a company in deep trouble. People tend to think of it as just being in television but it was in lots of other businesses, and in none of them was there a clear set of aims as to what success was going to be.

Therefore, we were flailing around in all sorts of ways. The first task for me was to get the half a dozen people who ran the key companies within Granada to sit down and simply lay out what they were actually trying to do. Without exception, they didn't know. And it's amazing how helpful it was to those who were up for it to then take on board what they were trying to do, so that at least everything they then did—and, more important, everything they asked other people to do—fit into that overall aim.

Starting a Business

We were bouncing around and around in circles. We didn't know whether we were in the catering business or the hotel business, or what we were trying to do in television. Were we trying to be the largest player in the ITV Network? We just didn't know. We just didn't have a clear vision of what we wanted. I'm almost reluctant to use the term *vision* because it's so abused. For me, vision is simple: a clear view of what it is that you're aiming to do.

As a leader I think it's important that you don't come up with all the ideas. You mustn't. In fact you can't come up with all the ideas. You must give people the task of clarifying for themselves what their vision for their part of the organization is. That's how you get buy-in: people feel it's theirs because it genuinely is in many cases, rather than being something that's given to them from above.

Of course, not everybody wants to buy into exactly what you want to do, and therefore it's important that together you have an open debate about where you might go and what the aims might be. But once you've had the debate, the decision must then be taken as to where you are going. Those who can't buy into it—and there will be very few, probably none—have to go somewhere else.

When you know where you want to go, you can't have people sitting in the organization who aren't prepared to go there with you. The lesson here is a simple one: be clear about what you and the organization are trying to do. Make it the first thing you do tomorrow morning. Actually sit down and ask yourself, "I'm running this part of the business. What am I trying to do?" If you do that, it's amazing how much easier life becomes.

TAKEAWAYS

⚵ If your business lacks clarity, it will be nearly impossible to get where you're trying to go.

Starting a Business

- ⚔ Sit down with key managers and map out a vision, with that vision simply being a clear view of what you are aiming to do.

- ⚔ Don't come up with all the ideas. Share with others the task of clarifying the vision. This, rather than handing down orders, is more likely to result in success.

- ⚔ Each day, ask yourself, "I'm running this. What am I trying to do?"

Aim Big,
Then Deliver

Luke Johnson

Chairman, Channel Four Television Corporation

FOR ME, IT'S IMPORTANT in business to be ambitious and to aim big. I think that sometimes in the past I was not ambitious enough. I keep trying to push myself harder to achieve more.

An example of this was four years ago when we started Strada, which is our chain of wood-fired pizzerias. We began with the idea that we would make it a big chain rather than just an individual, perfectly formed restaurant. So right from the beginning we were working out what would appeal and what we could replicate, rather than a simple, unique location. At each stage I'm forever pushing my partners to be more ambitious and take on more sites, as long as they're right. We'll find the money, we'll find the people, and the customers will come.

Clearly, you're forever trying to refine the concept and perfect it. And you must take the attitude that it's never going to be quite 100 percent; you can always do better. But in the meantime, while the new openings are being successful, we should aim to have a national business. In four years we've opened twenty-five restaurants, and things so far are going well.

Balancing the need to aim big with the day-to-day is always a challenge, and it's something you deal with on a weekly basis. Should we hire a new chef, or should we stick with our current chef, who costs less but isn't perhaps as imaginative? Should we start using different suppliers that are geared up to supply more restaurants? Should we take on more expensive software systems that can cope with multiple units?

All of these detailed decisions are an everyday occurrence. And if you have limited capital, it's sometimes a good constraint, because you can spend only what you have. However, the number of businesses that go through growing pains because they weren't ambitious enough early on about the premises they took on, or in taking out patents, or in dealing with their IT hiccups, is huge. It shows that if you are ambitious, you should always take on people who are slightly better than you can afford and space that gives you slightly more room than you need so that you can grow into it. I think, in general, that's a good thing, because business and life are about growth and progress, and you have to aim high.

The secret of business is how to turn an idea into a thriving business. Everyone has ideas; it's the translation and action that make the difference. This is one of the common errors of people who think the idea is what matters.

The idea is not what matters; what matters is putting it into action. That's difficult and boring and generally takes longer and costs more than one would like, and it's fraught with setbacks and blind alleys. But that's what makes the difference. So if I could have a thousand pounds for every new food restaurant concept that someone's put to me, I'd be a lot wealthier than I am. Ideas are easy.

We can all invent something like that, or we've all seen something that we think would replicate. It's the hard graft of recruiting the people, finding the suppliers, finding the site, fitting it out, and dealing with the health and safety and environmental planners and all the rest of it; funding the damn thing, coping with the start-up losses; dealing with customers day in, day out, and dealing with staff day in, day out. That's the reality of business. The big ideas are cheap.

TAKEAWAYS

- When starting a business, be ambitious, aim big, and push yourself to achieve more.

- Recognize that the secret of business is translating an idea and putting it into action.

- It is the hard, often boring work of putting an idea into action that makes all the difference.

- Hard work is the reality of business; big ideas are cheap.

Raising Money Is Like a Sales Process

Pamela Marrone

Founder and CEO,
Marrone Organic Innovations

ONE OF THE MOST ominous things that young entrepreneurs face when they're starting up a company is, how do I get money in the door? They see that as the biggest issue. And raising money seems to be a very difficult process.

For AgraQuest, which develops natural products for pest management, I raised $60 million, which is a lot of money in our business, because there are very few agricultural technology companies that have raised any money. [It's] very common in pharmaceutical, biotech, or software telecom, but not in our business. So everybody asks, "How in the world did you raise $60 million for an agricultural company?"

It's actually a very well-defined process, and it's just like sales. So a salesperson, a good one anyway, would have a contact list, and a way to manage that list—whether it's in an Excel spreadsheet or using some customer management software like Sales, Salesnet, or Salesforce.com. You have a pool of people that you're going to hit up as investors. And your list could be everybody you know.

You start with putting together whom you are going to target and then contact them. So it's like sales. Then you contact them; you make your pitch. And you must have a very good pitch. One of the key things is, can you pitch the company with passion, credibility? Can you clearly tell the investor what your company does, who your competitors are, what products you have, and how you are going to get to market; and how the investor is going to get money out of it? And who is your management team? So you have some very well-defined, concrete things that the investor wants to know, and you make a very clear, concise, and compelling pitch, just like you're selling something.

And so go out there; make your pitch. And do you always buy on the first pitch? No. I'm sure you don't always buy the first time someone tries to sell you something. You then have to follow up. You go back to your list—it comes up on your Outlook calendar that it's time to call so and so; it's been two weeks and you haven't heard from them—because they'll never call you back; you have to follow up with them. You get a little alert from your calendar and it says, "Call Mr. Investor, Prospect A." So you get on the phone and you call him.

Starting a Business

And you say, "We talked a couple of weeks ago, and what do you think?" Then, based on that conversation, if they are not ready to invest yet, you want to ask why. You want to get to a yes or no as quickly as possible, because what you'll find is that venture capitalists especially don't like to say no; they'll have you go and go and go, and put you off, and say they have to check with their partner or something.

So eight weeks or three months goes by and you still don't have a no. What you want to do is bring that investor to a no. Ask very concrete questions. Is this something that you can see yourself investing in? In what time frame do you think you can make a decision? How? What is the decision process for your firm? You want to get to that yes or no decision.

Again, I'm just illustrating a typical sales pipeline management type of position. Statistically they say that you have to talk to seven people before you get one sale. The key to raising money—and it's why I was successful—is to work really hard to get a lot of contacts, a big pool of investors who could possibly invest. So then if one drops out, you have another one waiting in the wings, and that's really the way it works.

TAKEAWAYS

⚔ Young entrepreneurs often find the task of getting money in the door to be very difficult. Raising money is actually a well-defined process, and it's just like sales.

⚔ To begin, create a pool of potential investors. Then contact those investors and make a clear, concise, and compelling pitch, one that includes passion and credibility.

⚔ Realize that not everyone will buy on the first pitch. In these cases, it's

Starting a Business

imperative to get to a yes or no answer
as quickly as possible.

꙰ Work hard to get a big pool of investors so that if one drops out, you
always have one waiting in the wings.

Treat Other People's Money As If It Were Your Own

Ray Anderson

Founder and Chairman, Interface, Inc.

OTHER PEOPLE'S MONEY; that's an interesting subject. When we began our company, I made the initial investment personally. And then friends came in, then a much larger partner joined in, and we eventually financed the company. And, by the way, the day we had our finance all in hand is the day we count as the birthday of Interface. Up to then, everything is conception and gestation, beginning with the gleam in my eye, perhaps the idea; but it's only when you have your money in hand that you can truly call yourself a company. And that's the birthday.

Interface, after getting through that treacherous start-up, in the teeth of the worst recession since 1929, really hit a home run year after year after year, 70 percent compound growth. And then ten years later we went public, and for the first time we had access to other people's money. Investors who bought shares in the stock, our expanded capital base of Interface, enabled us to begin to make acquisitions, and we made acquisitions in Canada, in Northern Ireland, and eventually in the United Kingdom and in Holland. And then in 1998, when the company was fifteen years old, we were a global company. Then we made other acquisitions, made subsequent stock offerings to the public, and had people subscribe to the stock and further expand the capital base, which enabled us to do more. We leveraged other people's money time and again over the years, so much so that it got to be a little too easy to access it.

And then we began a concentrated series of acquisitions to create a downstream distribution system. We made twenty-nine acquisitions, over a very short period of time, of contract dealers, the people who install and maintain their products. We wanted a captive, owned distribution system, and we invested $150 million of other people's money, basically by selling stock and doing bond offerings. And it was too easy.

If we'd been spending our own money, we would have thought very hard about those acquisitions. In the long run, they turned out to be a mistake, and six, seven years later we began to dismantle this distribution system and liquidate it, selling the businesses back to the owners or back to the employees. And we might not ever have undertaken that unfortunate series of investments if we'd been investing our own money. We would have questioned it.

Nothing will drive home the magnitude of a mistake like that the way a recession will. And our industry is just emerging from the deepest, most protracted recession in its history. Our primary marketplace, the American office market, declined 36 percent from peak to trough between 2001 and 2004. Imagine revenues drying up to that extent—the entire marketplace, not just us. In fact, we were down less than the total marketplace. We were gaining market share in the midst of this, but it was nevertheless a scary time for us. And that imposes a discipline on you. You look at the superfluous stuff that you've accumulated using other people's money, and you divest it; you cut your losses as best you can. It's a sobering lesson. And the marketplace itself instills that discipline in you, too.

We'll think twice before we make an acquisition or series of acquisitions like that again, however easy it is to access other people's money. The objective ought to be to treat other people's money as if it were your own.

TAKEAWAYS

- ⚏ When you have money in hand, you can truly call yourself a company. But beware. If leveraging investors' money seems too easy, it is.

- ⚏ Question those decisions that involve money to avoid making bad investments.

- ⚏ If you find yourself in trouble, cut your losses as best you can.

- ⚏ Ultimately, the objective is to treat other people's money as if it were your own.

The Birth
of BET

Robert Johnson

Founder, Black Entertainment Television

THE WAY I GOT into the cable industry,
which eventually led to the launch of Black
Entertainment Television (BET), was that
I'd been working on Capitol Hill as a press
secretary. I decided I wanted to get into business because it was one experience I'd never
had. I'd worked at the Urban League, and
I'd worked at the Corporation for Public

Starting a Business

Broadcasting, but I had no business experience. Just as serendipity would have it, I happened to be at a cocktail party at my next-door neighbor's house, and she said, "You'd make a great lobbyist for the cable industry." I didn't know anything about cable, and I said so. She said, "Don't worry. I didn't know anything about it when I got in it. You'll do all right."

My neighbor introduced me to the head of the cable trade association, and he offered me a job as a lobbyist for the cable industry. Through that experience I got a chance to meet all of the pioneers of the cable industry: Ted Turner, who was a member of the board of directors; John Malone, who was head of a company called TCI at the time; Jerry Levin of Home Box Office; and Ralph Baruch of Viacom. All the major cable industry leaders. So I got to know them, and I had a chance to meet John Malone.

One day John said to me, "Bob, if you have any ideas about business, come talk to me." So after I decided I wanted to do BET, the first person I went to talk to was John

Starting a Business

Malone. I remember going out and presenting the idea of a cable channel to target African Americans. John asked me how much it would cost to launch this. I said that it would probably cost about half a million dollars. All of this took place within about a thirty-minute conversation, and John said, "Bob, I'll tell you what I'll do. I like what you're doing, because we have a small cable system in Memphis. We have minority subscribers that I think would help us in our franchising, in our marketing. I'll buy 20 percent of your company for 180, and I'll loan you 320. That will be your $500,000; and I'll be 20 percent of the company, and you'll be 80 percent. Is that a deal?" I said, "John, that's a deal." What Malone didn't know was, at the time if he'd reversed the numbers and said, "I'll be 80 and you'll be 20," I would have said, "John, that's a deal." But he didn't do that, so I ended up with 80 percent of BET, $500,000 of John's money. He ended up with 20 percent.

He gave me a check for $500,000. This was more money than I'd ever seen in my entire life. I grew up in a family of ten kids in a small town, and it was probably more money than all the black families in the town had, combined. So he gave me the money, and I said, "John, I've never run a business. What advice can you give me?" He said, "Bob, it's very simple. Get your revenues up; keep your costs down." And after that, that was my mantra for running a business: make sure you have more money coming in than you're spending.

Look at your business model and see where you can find a source of content or product that will enable you to control your costs, because your revenue is not predictable. We had to get cable operators to carry us; many cable operators didn't have African Americans in their marketplace. We had to get advertisers to spend. Advertisers regarded cable, when it was in its infancy, in the early eighties when BET was starting, as not a very attractive medium because it was up against the huge broadcast networks, local TV, and local radio. It was the new kid on the block. It wasn't even like magazines and newspapers.

Starting a Business

I had to focus on finding a cost basis that
would be consistent with unpredictable revenue. And programming content that was
free was the best cost basis in the world,
naturally. So when the record companies
started to use cable—they started with MTV
principally—as a way of promoting their
artists, they would give the videos to the
cable programming channels for free in
return for the promotion. So you had a
content base that was free, but you had
two sources of income: cable operators
and advertisers. It was one of the best business models in the world—low-cost content, two streams of revenue. That taught
me very quickly that if you can control your
costs, maximize your revenue, and build
margins based on that, you have a very successful business model. And then layer on
that a brand that becomes an accepted icon
within the community. BET became that
brand. It was a brand built on delivering
entertainment at low cost to consumers and
having advertising and cable operators pay
for it.

TAKEAWAYS

⊰ Even when you don't know much about business, a desire to experience it can take an entrepreneur far.

⊰ When running a business, follow this simple mantra: make sure you have more money coming in than you're spending.

⊰ Because revenue is not predictable, it's important to look at your business model and find a source of content or product that will enable you to control costs.

⊰ Once a successful business model is in place, start building your brand within the community.

How Small Businesses Can Compete for Talent

Andrew Sherman

Cofounder and CEO,
Grow Fast Grow Right

Starting a Business

ONE OF THE THINGS that really strikes me as I look at the challenges of small, growing companies nationwide or world-wide is how they can attract and compete for human capital when there are so many larger companies and global companies to compete against when it comes to pay, compensation, and career track.

A story that we recently encountered was a company that had a lot of trouble compet-ing for talent with a company in the same industry that was literally across the street. And what they really—I call them the whin-ers—were always whining about was "We're losing this manager to this person. We're losing that manager to this person. What are we going to do? We can't pay the same. Our overhead needs to be lower."

And what was ultimately happening was that the company was failing to understand its cultural value proposition. I think the takeaway lesson there is: understand why people come to work for you in the first place. What kinds of things can you do to keep them, and what types of more creative benefits packages can you develop?

It turns out that there were some things about the company that people really liked. The leadership of the company had set a certain tone and had been doing certain things, and they had abandoned those things in trying to look more like the bigger company. By returning to its roots—in terms of its culture, its compensation, the way the leaders interacted with people, the way people dealt with each other, and the respect they had for each other—the company was able to hold on to people a lot longer and actually pay them less than the competitor.

[There are] several takeaway lessons from the story. This company had grown to $100 million in revenues and had still not hired a senior vice president of human resources. We had a real heart-to-heart about what that meant—having that many people working in the company, coming in every day, not really taking the time to understand why people were working there, what they found compelling. The company needed to state the cultural value proposition more clearly and then tie it back to recruitment.

They felt like they were spending a lot of time with existing employees talking about their culture, but then they were not funneling that knowledge into a recruitment strategy. They had no position descriptions at the senior level. They'd lost touch with some of the creative and fun culture that they had built.

The company is going through a move to new facilities, from one neighborhood to a more downtown setting, and they are just beginning to study the cultural impact that the move would have. It's all these little things. When a small company is trying to stay competitive, it can't overlook the small things. It may be those small things that the employees find compelling in the first place and where employees are willing to sacrifice dollars in exchange.

You ask the average employee, "Which would you rather have, a 10 percent raise in

your pay or a 20 to 30 percent raise in the
enjoyableness of your work environment?"
Many of them will choose the latter over the
former because that 10 percent increase in
pay after taxes is nowhere near the health
and happiness and smiles on their faces and
their looking forward to going to work as a
compromise. [It isn't as valuable as the leaders of the company] having an open-door
policy, walking the talk, walking the halls,
and just going around and saying, "Hey,
you did a great job today, and let me tell you
why. I just got a call from a customer." Many
people want recognition more than they
want dollars. They need dollars to pay bills,
but emotionally and psychologically they
want recognition for a job well done.

In a small company you can take advantage of the fact the leader and owner of the
company might be just down the hall or one
floor away instead of a thousand miles away
or completely unreachable. Many small
companies, while they're whining about
their inability to retain employees, are losing

sight of what brought employees to their company in the first place.

TAKEAWAYS

⚔ Leaders of small companies face a challenge in attracting and competing for human capital when it comes to pay, compensation, and career track.

⚔ To compete for and retain talent, you must understand why people come to work for you.

⚔ No matter how you grow, remember your roots—your cultural value proposition—and tie that into recruitment efforts.

Starting a Business

⚔ Many people want recognition more
than they want dollars. Don't lose sight
of the small things or what brought
employees to your door in the first
place.

Only Hire People You Like

Mike Southon

Chairman, Beermat Ecademy

DREAM TEAMS [can exist] up to about 150 people, we reckon, because there are some magic numbers, which we've learned from experience. From 10-25 people, you have a certain atmosphere; between 25 and 35 you move from being a small company to a big company. But you can keep the tribal atmosphere up to about 150.

The Instruction Set, when we sold it, had 150 people. We reckon we had one entrepreneur, four cornerstones, and a 145-person dream team. We only made three or four mistakes along the way, and that was because we hired people against our better judgment. We talked ourselves into it. They had the technical skills, but they were a bit strange. We thought they'd work out, but no, they didn't. Your instincts are always right.

We used to have a recruitment regime where you'd meet somebody first and see if they had the basic skills. Or if they were a friend of yours, they obviously got a short-cut. Then it was meet everybody, and if one person didn't like you, we didn't hire you. In reality it wasn't always like that; it was always everybody hated or everybody liked them. [We used to say,] "Take them down the pub and put a couple of drinks into them," which is not very PC to say, but after a couple of drinks you find out what people are like.

Starting a Business

I remember one story when the Instruction Set got to about twenty-five people, and I was running sales. I hadn't really done sales before. I thought, "I'd better hire a grown-up." So I went to a recruitment agency and these CVs arrived—people with fantastic credentials. There was one particular gentleman, and his motto was "Give me the bullets, and I'll fire them," because he said he'd doubled revenue everywhere he'd been. So I thought he was a good guy. He came in, extended a big handshake, made eye contact, and said, "Yes, give me the bullets; I'll fire them. Michael, I'll double your revenue. That's what I do."

So I asked him to meet everybody. His body language with different people was fun. With all the ladies, he was staring at the cleavage. With other directors, it was the big handshake and "Give me the bullets; I'll fire them." I thought that must be what salesmen are like. Then I took him to lunch, and the waitress made some error—I can't remember what it was—and he tore off a strip of her in front of me, to show me how tough he was. I thought, "What an idiot."

I went back to the office and thought, that's what you have to do; you hire people like that. And I decided that no, I was not hiring him; the man's an idiot. People were knocking on my door, asking what I thought of the guy. And I said, "Sorry, I should hire him because he's brilliant and he'd double our revenue, but I didn't like him, so I'm not hiring him." They said, "Thank God for that. We all thought he was an idiot as well."

So instincts were right. I sent him an e-mail saying that I was really sorry, that we were a bit strange at the Instruction Set, that we didn't behave like normal companies, and that he'd probably be brilliant else-where, but here he wouldn't be perfect, but best of luck. I got a week of abusive e-mails from him. Then I remembered that his CV said that he doubled revenue everywhere he'd been, but nobody—because I called to check—said they liked him.

Starting a Business

Only hire people you like, because what's the point of hiring people you don't like? Sometimes in large companies we're forced to work with people we don't like, and that's hell. You don't need to do it in a start-up.

———•◦•———

TAKEAWAYS

———•◦•———

⚷ In a start-up, don't hire someone against your better judgment, and don't talk yourself into it.

⚷ Trust your instincts. A candidate may have technical savvy, but if his or her personality isn't a fit, it won't work out.

⚷ Introduce job candidates to others in the office, and then watch how they interact with others and how others interact with them.

Starting a Business

⚶ In large companies, people have to work with people they don't like and it's "hell"; you don't need to do it in a start-up.

Building Brand Awareness

Sir Stelios Haji-Ioannou

Founder, easyGroup

IN MY EXPERIENCE the cheapest and quickest way of building a brand without massive advertising budgets is to use an individual: to have a face for the company.

People are interested in people; newspapers and media generally tend to talk about people rather than companies. So if there is a human-interest story somewhere, if there is someone who can spearhead the brand, it's bound to be cheaper and easier to brand-build. And pick an enemy; choose a company—hopefully a household name—that you can pick a fight with.

For example, when I started easyJet in 1995, obviously nobody had heard of the company. It was an uphill struggle in the first couple of years. Then British Airways decided to enter the market and pick a fight with us by creating Go, a company that easyJet plc subsequently bought.

Back in 1997 and 1998 it was a useful and convenient story to have out in the media that easyJet was so successful and making such a difference in the European aviation market and people's lives that even British Airways, the almighty "world's favorite airline," had to imitate it. The fact that I was personally present on Go's inaugural flight, wearing an orange jumpsuit, hijacked the media opportunity in our favor.

We were not the only low-cost airline back then. It's interesting that we coexisted with companies like Ryanair, which is obviously still around, and companies like Debonair, which is not. But it was our ability to grab the opportunity and become the archrival of British Airways that elevated easyJet above the rivals and other smaller, low-cost airlines that made it a household name in Britain in just a couple of years.

———◆———

TAKEAWAYS

———◆———

- ⚎ Without a massive advertising budget, the cheapest and quickest way to build a brand is to use an individual. Put a face on your company.

- ⚎ Because people are interested in other people, use human-interest stories as a cheap and easy way to build brand.

- ⚎ Then find an enemy—preferably a household name—with whom you can pick a fight. Consider hijacking their PR events that are relevant to your brand.

⚔ Small companies can become household names simply by grabbing opportunities and becoming archrivals of their competitors.

——◆◆◆——

Never Take No for an Answer

——◆◆◆——

Brent Hoberman

Cofounder, CSO, and Chairman,
Lastminute.com

I THINK TENACITY for me is just never saying no, and I think that is what every entrepreneur will have many examples of—where they've had to overcome obstacles.

Starting a Business

For Lastminute.com, one of the biggest lessons was actually getting the original domain name. We didn't own it—a lot of people don't realize that when Martha [Lane Fox, cofounder] and I went to twenty venture capitalists to try and raise money, we didn't actually own the domain name.

So they put money into a business plan that was just called Last Minute Network Limited, because we weren't able—prior to raising the money—to buy the domain name. And even once we'd raised it, I kept calling the guy whom I bought it from, and he kept saying no. It took four calls. I think a lot of people would probably give up after the third call. In buying the initial domain name, it was a lot about who owned it, finding out and doing research on the Internet, and then calling the guy.

Trying to find out how much money he was making from the initial domain name was a large part of it, so the negotiation for me very much stemmed around [his] renting the domain name to a German magazine called *Focus*. He was just bartering it; he was getting customers for his small Internet service provider.

What I then kept saying to him was "Well, you wouldn't spend money, you wouldn't value it in that way, you wouldn't actually give them that much cash, because it's not a very efficient place for you to advertise."

He agreed with that, and I knew I had something, so I started talking real cash. That was what obviously grabbed his attention. At the time we raised £600,000 and so to spend even £16,000 for just a domain name seemed like quite a lot. But we knew equally that the name would be extremely powerful and that not to have it with the Lastminute.com service we were going to provide would be a major disadvantage.

We had to have it, and in the end it was just the balance of the deal, the way it was structured. It was also a negotiation style that was quite friendly and not aggressive; I think that probably helped as well.

All the way along we've had examples of tenacity. One of them would be getting airlines on board in the early days, or getting the Savoy Group, for example, which was a wonderful supplier for us. In the early days they just said, "No, no, no!" I got hold of the mobile phone numbers of various people and just kept calling, and I think it became less hassle for them just to give us product than to keep getting the calls.

It really is just not taking no for an answer. It is ensuring that you are still looking at the issues and you can be pragmatic enough to see that the obstacles can be overcome. It is definitely never accepting no as a first answer —maybe once you have it ten, twenty, thirty times, you have to start thinking about it.

It's also setting goals. I remember one of the first bits of advice we got when we were first trying to raise money was to set ourselves a deadline. Somebody said, "Look, if you haven't raised money in eight months or whatever it is, just give up."

So there is tenacity, but there is also knowing when you really are hitting your head against a brick wall. But to find that out you have to hit your head several times against that wall.

TAKEAWAYS

- ☙ Entrepreneurs must be tenacious. They should never take no for an answer.

- ☙ Keep calling whenever you are faced with a "no" but continue to look at the issues and the obstacles to be overcome.

- ☙ Never, ever accept "no" as a first answer. Only if you encounter "no" ten or twenty or thirty times should you even think about it.

- ☙ Be tenacious, but be willing to recognize when you really are hitting your head against a brick wall.

— ▪◆▪ —

Overcoming Obstacles

— ▪◆▪ —

Lord Bilimoria

Founder and CEO, Cobra Beer

ON THE JOURNEY of building a brand
you come across lots of obstacles, and the
word you get used to more than anything
else is *no*. When you try and sell, when you
try and persuade people to invest in you, or
try to raise finances, it's always *no*. Really,
what one's got to do is get to the other side
of those obstacles. Whether you go through

them, under them, around them or over
them, you have to get to the other side; and
one of the secrets is to turn those obstacles
into advantages.

I'll never forget in the early days when we
went to the brewery in India and we said,
"What we really need is 330-mL small bottles and draft beer because that's what the
market in the U.K. is used to." And the
brewer replied, "Well, we produce one size
bottle, which is a 660-mL bottle, and this is
a standard beer bottle in which virtually all
beer in India is produced. Every brewery
uses this standard shape and size of bottle,
that's what our production lines are geared
up to, and we don't think you stand a chance
anyway. So you must have it produced in
this size and shape of bottle. And forget
draft beer; we're not going to send kegs all
the way to England and have empty kegs
coming all the way back to India; it's not
going to be practical." So we said, "OK, this
is all we have."

It was a real problem, a real barrier. We
used to go around to the restaurants door to

door in our battered old Citroën 2CV with
our beer, park a little bit ahead, and carry
this beer across to the restaurant owners
and say, "Here we are; fantastic, authentic
Indian beer; try it."

Of course, another obstacle was that a lot
of them would say, "Sorry, we don't drink."
Over two-thirds of the Indian restaurants
in the U.K. are actually owned or run by
Bangladeshis who are Muslims. The others
are owned or run by Pakistanis, Indians, Sri
Lankans, Nepalese. So a lot of them, for
religious reasons, don't drink. I learned a
fundamental lesson there that it doesn't
matter that we don't drink; it's our customers that matter. They said, "Leave a
couple of bottles; we'll try it out with our
regular customers. If they like it we'll put in
our first order, and if our wider customers
like it we'll reorder." I'll never forget the
support that the Indian restaurateurs gave
us, which is why we are where we are today.

They'd also say, "It's all very well you saying your beer's great, but how are we going
to sell it in these huge 660-mL bottles?

Starting a Business

Give us some small bottles of draft." Of course we couldn't, so we replied, "Well, actually, do you realize that this 660-mL bottle is exactly double the size of a 330-mL bottle? So every time you sell one of these to your customers you'll be selling double the amount of beer. Then you're going to be selling them authentic Indian beer, with authentic Indian packaging in the way that beer is sold in India. And because they're double-size bottles, the waiting staff can leave them on the table and customers can help themselves.

"Also, much in the way that customers share Indian food and order lots for the table and people try out different dishes, you can leave the big bottles on the table and people can share them—so you create a sharing environment. And what's further is that people at other tables will see these bottles and say, 'They look like bottles of wine, but they're not bottles of wine—what are they? Oh, they're bottles of beer.' And it spreads like wildfire around a restaurant."

Starting a Business

So we turned this huge obstacle of a giant beer bottle into a big advantage, and now the majority of our sales are in the 660-mL beer bottles. When we started producing Cobra Beer in the U.K. in 1997, we produced the first 660-mL bottle in Britain. Today if you go into a supermarket you will see virtually every major international beer brand available in Britain is also available in 660-mL beer bottles, and we were the pioneers of that.

When being faced with obstacles and threats, the most important thing is always to have the attitude "I'm going to get to the other side; I'm going to turn this obstacle into an opportunity; I'm going to turn this threat into an opportunity."

TAKEAWAYS

- ⚔ When building a brand, you will come across many obstacles, and the word you get used to more than any other is *no*.

- ⚔ Whether you go through, under, around, or over the obstacles, you have to get to the other side.

- ⚔ Turn obstacles and threats into advantages.

- ⚔ Above all, always have the attitude "I'm going to get to the other side; I'm going to turn this obstacle into an opportunity."

————◆◆◆————

Rising from
the Ashes After
a Crisis

Ping Fu

Chairman, President, and CEO, Geomagic

————◆◆◆————

MY GREATEST CHALLENGE was in the
beginning of 2001, when the company was
given back to me and I became a CEO. I was
a cofounder before and the company, after
raising the venture capital money, hired a
management team. The company raised the

money at a time when the Internet was very hot, and during that time it was very fashionable to bring in seasoned managers. Entrepreneurs usually are considered not very good businesspeople. So I stepped down as a CTO.

But two years down the road that didn't work, and the Internet bubble crashed. As a founder of the company, I was left, basically, to steer the ship. There was no one else in the management team left at the time when the company was going to die.

Well, the situation was far worse than I expected, and I was shell-shocked when the CEO told me, "Ping, I have bad news for you. The company's going to run out of cash in three months, and there's no chance that we're going to survive. And more than that, I'm leaving, and the VP of sales is leaving, so you are going to be left with the company. You can decide whatever you want to do with it since it's your baby."

I felt, first of all, a profound sense of failure, because I was part of the management team, too. Their failure was my failure. That was my first reaction. The second was fear: Oh, my God; I raised the money—my own money, my family's money, the investors' money. They trusted me. The early people were friends of mine or students of my husband. They trusted me. Now I had to tell them that their money was down the gutter and that they didn't have a job. I panicked.

But then it didn't take very long. We had the meeting in the morning, and by the evening I'd told myself, "Well, the situation is what it is. There is nothing I can do by being shocked or being panicked. I've got to have a plan. I've got to do something."

The first thing is open communication—silence always brews distrust. So the very first thing I did was go to the board and tell them that I was willing to take over the company and would stay with the company and do whatever was best with what was left over. I would try to save the company, and if I could not, I would try to sell the company so that they could get some investment back.

Starting a Business

The second thing to do was to communicate with the employees and clearly tell them what the situation was, why I needed their help, and how much cash we had left. And then I told them I would survive because I have always been a survivor. I had gone through very tough situations when I was in China—in the crisis is when I shine. I asked them to stay with me, trust me, and help me through the difficult times. So you give them open communication, and you ask for help.

Other than that, I knew I needed to get cash and get cash fast. I couldn't worry about whether or not the business deal that I was doing was the best deal or not. I couldn't worry about whether it was a right or wrong decision—getting the deal to give me the cash was what was going to help us survive.

I went after a large customer, which was Align Technology. They make Invisalign— the corrective for teeth without wires and brackets. They were [thinking] about an IPO, and I offered the technology to them. Now if we were in good condition, I probably could have negotiated a better deal that sustained the revenue to this day. But I sold the technology to them for cash, so we got very quick cash. They felt it was a fantastic deal for them. The technology was exactly what they needed to go public. And for me [the goal] was to get $2 million within three months—where can you get it? So I got that deal. They were happy, and I got what I needed to float the company.

Once we got the cash in place, morale was higher, and employees started to trust me more because I had delivered what I said I could deliver. By then we had not just three months of cash but a year of cash.

The first strategy for a situation like this is: do not run out of cash. And then what I did was hire a really good sales executive to come in to help me sell the software. Knowing what failed the last team, I had a better idea of whom I needed to hire. In some ways failure is never a failure; it can always serve as a good example to teach you what you need to do better next time.

Starting a Business

What happened to the company is that we were able to achieve positive cash flow at the end of the first year, profitability at the end of the second year, and by the end of the fifth year we had grown more than 2,000 percent, during most difficult economic conditions.

I think to rise from the ashes you must keep a very cool, collected head because everybody's watching you. You must keep high integrity and remove any distrust that can possibly happen during the crisis because that's what's happening, emotions are running high—you must, must do that. And then you must be very clear-headed on a single strategy to survive and then execute on that. You don't have a lot of time to wander around.

TAKEAWAYS

- As an entrepreneur, one of your greatest challenges may be to steer a ship in troubled waters. Don't panic.

- Start with open communication. Talk honestly with investors and employees about the situation, and ask for help.

- Most importantly, do not allow the business to run out of cash.

- To rise from the ashes after a crisis, remain cool and collected, maintain high integrity, and execute on a single strategy.

—◆◆◆—

Prove
Your Concept
Before
Expanding

—◆◆◆—

Robin Chase

Founder and Former CEO,
Zipcar

Starting a Business

ZIPCAR WAS CREATED right on the heels of the dot-com bust, and I was constantly trying to reflect on what happened. I feel, particularly when you take venture money, there's a huge pressure to expand really quickly.

That is fine for those venture capitalists who have ten companies and they're only expecting one of the ten to win; but we, as CEOs and as business people, actually want our one to succeed. And part of that success is not expanding before you can handle that expansion.

I thought that there were a huge number of companies that expanded across markets or stores before the business model or the operational model had been worked out. So it's really easy to get yourself into a completely chaotic state very quickly if you spring up before you're ready.

Think about what the critical things are that you have to understand—the revenue model, the operations, and how to market—before you expand. And once you nail that, then you can expand quickly and even do trial expansions so that you really have understood what it's going to take and what things you might not have spotted, and then you can do the big expansion.

In Zipcar, with my first seed capital money, I knew that I needed to do the proof of concept in Boston. And that proof of concept was that the technology would work, the operations would be smooth, and there was some sort of demand. But I didn't think I had to prove the demand in that first year and a half, because marketing, as we know, was incredibly expensive in general. And I didn't have that kind of wherewithal to spend money in marketing and prove this technology and operational piece.

We expanded into Washington when I felt quite secure that we could service the cars remotely and do customer service remotely, and that there were some economies of scale. Moving to Washington was the proof that our systems were scalable. I staggered that by four months with opening in New

York City, similarly, so I could learn something from that Washington opening and then take it to New York.

And we did learn. We learned a lot about marketing and positioning of the cars—how to expand in that first burst. So staggered learning on these very high-risk things is very important.

TAKEAWAYS

- ⊰ Whenever you take venture money, there is a huge pressure to expand the business quickly.

- ⊰ To succeed, entrepreneurs must not expand until the business can handle that expansion.

Starting a Business

⊰ First get a handle on the revenue model, operations, and marketing. Then do trial expansions and work on your proof of concept.

⊰ Staggering your learning on high-risk ventures is extremely important.

Do What You Love

Howard Lester

Chairman and CEO,
Williams–Sonoma

I GOT INTO THIS BUSINESS and it was kind of an interesting period in my life. I'd grown up in the computer services and software business, had finally sold the company, and was living in Southern California and loafing, playing golf. I started feeling like a degenerate. I was only in my early forties and just didn't have anything to do. All of my friends were working, so I couldn't even find anybody to have lunch with.

I started thinking a lot about what I wanted to do and what was going to make me happy, and I realized that to that point in my working career, I had kind of done the things that were necessary. I was trying to make a living and just do the best I could and make money, but I was never really happy. I wasn't excited about getting out of bed in the morning and going to work, so I gave a lot of thought to what it was that I wanted to do, and I knew it was something different.

One of the main conclusions that I reached was that it was important for me at that point in my life—as I mentioned, I was in my early forties—to do something; you know, this is not a dress rehearsal. And I wanted to do things that I loved doing. Why go through life doing things that you don't love doing? And I felt that if I was doing something I loved, I'd have a better chance at being good at it than doing something that I didn't love, because it wouldn't be work, it would be joy.

So I went on a little journey of looking at a lot of businesses, some of them pretty weird. And one day I came across this little company called Williams-Sonoma, which was struggling. It was a little $4 million company with four stores and a small catalog, located in San Francisco. One thing led to another, and I was able to purchase the business in the summer of 1978.

We've been very fortunate. We've grown a business that we're quite proud of, and I can tell you that since acquiring Williams-Sonoma, I don't think there has been a day or a morning when I wasn't excited about getting up and going to work. I've loved what we do, I've loved our customers, and I've loved our merchandise. I'm so proud of what we do. Every time I walk into a store, pick up a catalog, or look on the Internet, I'm just so proud of our people and what our customers say about us. It's been a wonderful experience for me.

TAKEAWAYS

- ⚑ When you're no longer excited about getting out of bed in the morning, it's time to do something different.

- ⚑ Life is not a dress rehearsal. Do things that you love doing.

- ⚑ You'll have a better chance at being good at what you do if you find joy in it.

- ⚑ Loving what you do can be a wonderful experience.

✂ ABOUT THE ✂
CONTRIBUTORS

Ray Anderson is the founder and chairman of Interface, Inc., one of the world's largest interior furnishings companies. He is also the company's former president and CEO.

Mr. Anderson began his career in the carpeting and textile businesses while at Deering Milliken and Callaway Mills. In 1973 he founded Interface and began producing free-lay carpet tiles in the United States. In the same year, he also partnered with Carpets International in Britain, which he took over twenty years later.

Today, Interface is still a leader in its core business, modular soft-surfaced floor coverings. Mr. Anderson is recognized as one of the world's most environmentally progressive leaders, and Interface is known as a leader in the green business movement.

Mr. Anderson served as cochairman of the President's Council on Sustainable Development during the Clinton administration. He currently serves on the boards of Melaver, Inc.; the Georgia Conservancy; the Ida Cason Callaway Foundation; and Rocky Mountain Institute. He is an adviser for the University of Texas Center for Sustainable Development.

About the Contributors

Lord Bilimoria is the founder and CEO of Cobra Beer, a premier brewing company.

Lord Bilimoria started his career in 1982 at Ernst & Young, where he spent four years working in audit, tax, training, and accounting. He qualified as a chartered accountant in 1986 and graduated in law from Cambridge University in 1988. He then worked at Cresvale in London (part of S&W Beresford) as a consulting accountant.

In 1989 he moved to *European Accounting Focus* magazine as its Sales and Marketing Director. Later that year he founded Cobra Beer, realizing his ambition to develop a premium lager brewed to appeal to ale drinkers and lager drinkers alike.

Lord Bilimoria then extended into other markets with the launch of General Bilimoria Wines, and *Tandoori* magazine and Tandoorimagazine .com. He also founded Curryzone.com and is the founder and chairman of Cobrabyte Technologies.

He is a director of Brake Brothers and an advisory board member for Boston Analytics. In addition, Lord Bilimoria is chairman of the British government's National Employment Panel's Small and Medium-Sized Enterprise Board and vice chairman of the London Chamber of Commerce and Industry's Asian Business Association.

Robin Chase is the founder and former CEO of Zipcar, a company that offers car rentals by the hour. She is the founder and CEO of Meadow Networks.

In June 2000, Ms. Chase cofounded Zipcar, a car-sharing service that allows members to rent cars

About the Contributors

online for short periods. She stepped down as CEO in 2003, at which point she founded and became CEO of Meadow Networks, a consultancy that applies wireless technologies to transportation. She also founded GoLoco, a ride-sharing service.

Ms. Chase is a frequent lecturer and has been featured on the *Today* show and National Public Radio and in the *New York Times* and *Wired* and *Time* magazines.

She currently serves on the National Smart Growth Council, the Kyoto Cities Initiative International Advisory Council, and the Boston Mayor's Wireless Task Force.

Michael Dell is the founder, CEO, and chairman of Dell, Inc., the direct-sale computer company he founded in 1984. He is also the author of *Direct from Dell: Strategies That Revolutionized an Industry.*

Mr. Dell started his computer company with $1,000 and a goal to build relationships directly with customers. By 1992 he had become the youngest CEO to earn a place among the Fortune 500. In 1998 he formed MSD Capital, a private investment firm. In 2001 Dell ranked number one in global market share.

Mr. Dell serves on the Foundation Board of the World Economic Forum and the executive committee of its International Business Council. He is a member of the U.S. Business Council. Mr. Dell also serves on the U.S. President's Council of Advisors

on Science and Technology and the governing board
of the Indian School of Business in Hyderabad,
India.

Ping Fu is chairman, president, and CEO of Geomagic, a global software and services company that
specializes in 3D technologies.

Prior to cofounding Geomagic, Ms. Fu was
Director of Visualization at the National Center
for Supercomputing Applications, where she ini-
tiated and managed the NCSA Mosaic software
project, which led to the development of Netscape
and Internet Explorer. She has more than twenty
years of software industry experience in database,
networking, geometry processing, and computer
graphics.

In 1982 Ms. Fu cofounded Geomagic. Since
then she has led the company from a small start-up
to a global leader in digital shape sampling and processing (DSSP).

In 2005, Ms. Fu was named Entrepreneur of the
Year by *Inc.* magazine.

Sir Stelios Haji-Ioannou is the founder of easy-
Group, the private holding company that creates
new ventures and owns the "easy" brand.

After graduation from London's City University
Business School in shipping and finance, Sir Stelios
joined his father's company, Troodos Shipping.
He founded his first venture, Stelmar Tankers, in

1992. Three years later he started easyJet, of which he is still the largest single shareholder.

In 1998 he formed the holding company easy-Group to explore new ventures to extend the "easy" brand. He remains chairman of each business. Among others, easyGroup includes easyInternetcafe, easyCar, easyMoney, easyCinema, and easyCruise.

Sir Stelios is also the founding chairman of CYMEPA, the Cyprus Marine Environment Protection Association.

Brent Hoberman is the cofounder of Lastminute .com, the travel and leisure Web site purchased by Travelocity Europe in 2005. He currently serves as chairman and chief strategy officer.

Mr. Hoberman spent five years consulting at Mars & Co. and Spectrum Strategy Consultants, where he specialized in media and telecoms. He has always had an interest in the latest innovations in technology. Prior to starting Lastminute.com, he was a founding member and Head of Business Development at QXL, and he also worked in business development at LineOne.

Mr. Hoberman cofounded Lastminute.com in April 1998. His key priority was maintaining and developing the company's relationship with key stakeholders, including the financial community, shareholders, and customers. Lastminute.com was sold to Travelocity (Sabre Holdings) in 2005.

Mr. Hoberman joined the Guardian Media Group in January 2007 as a director.

About the Contributors

Luke Johnson is chairman of Channel Four Television Corporation, a leading publicly owned broadcaster in the United Kingdom.

Mr. Johnson first showed his interest in business when he started running nightclubs while studying medicine at Oxford. He then joined Kleinwort Benson, the investment bank, as an analyst.

In 1993 he organized the acquisition of Pizza-Express and floated the business on the stock market at 40P. He was its chairman until 1999, at which time the share price was over 900P. In 1999 Mr. Johnson started Signature Restaurants, which included the Belgo chain. After selling the business in 2005, he started the Strada chain, which he sold in late 2005 after expanding the chain to thirty units. He currently serves as chairman.

Mr. Johnson became chairman of Channel Four Television in January 2004 and continues to serve in that role. Since 2000 he has been a leading investor in a number of public and private companies, and he continues to be in his capacity as chairman of the private investment vehicle Risk Capital Partners.

Mr. Johnson is also a director of Elderstreet VCT, a venture capital fund management company, and InterQuest Group, an IT staffing solutions group.

Robert Johnson is the founder of Black Entertainment Television (BET), a cable television network targeted to African Americans. He is also

the founder, chairman, and CEO of the RLJ
Companies.

During his early career Mr. Johnson worked for
the Corporation for Public Broadcasting and the
Washington Urban League. He also worked as press
secretary for Walter Fauntroy, the congressional
delegate from Washington, D.C.

In 1976 Mr. Johnson became Vice President of
Government Relations for the National Cable &
Telecommunications Association. He left this posi-
tion in 1979 to start Black Entertainment Televi-
sion, which began broadcasting for the first time in
January 1980.

In 1991 the company went public, but in 1998
Mr. Johnson took the company private once more
before selling it to Viacom in 1999. Mr. Johnson
stayed on as chairman and CEO until 2005.

Mr. Johnson is the founder of RLJ Companies,
a business network that provides strategic investment and direction in and for the financial services,
real estate, hospitality/restaurant, professional
sports, film production, gaming, and recording in-
dustries. He currently serves as chairman and CEO.

In addition, Mr. Johnson serves on the follow-
ing boards of directors: NBA Board of Governors;
Lowe's Companies, Inc.; International Management Group (IMG); American Film Institute;
Strayer Education, Inc.; Johns Hopkins University;
the Business Council; Wal-Mart Advisory Council;
and Deutsche Bank Advisory Board. He is a former
director of Hilton Hotels Corporation.

About the Contributors

Howard Lester is the chairman and CEO of Williams-Sonoma, a premier specialty retailer of home furnishings.

Mr. Lester has extensive experience in computer operations and spent fifteen years in the computer industry before entering retailing. He spent six years with Computer Sciences Corporation and then became executive vice president of Bradford National Corporation, which had acquired Centurex.

Mr. Lester purchased Williams-Sonoma in 1978, and since that time he has held the positions of president, CEO, and now chairman.

Mr. Lester is also on the board of Harold's Stores and is on the Executive Council of the University of California, San Francisco. He is on the advisory boards of the Retail Management Institute of Santa Clara University and the Walter A. Haas School of Business at the University of California, Berkeley.

Pamela Marrone is the founder and CEO of Marrone Organic Innovations. She is the founder and former CEO of AgraQuest, Inc. Both companies are natural pest management companies.

From 1983 to 1989 Ms. Marrone led the insect biology group at Monsanto, developing novel solutions for controlling insects. In 1990 she left to become founding president of Entotech, Inc., a biopesticide subsidiary of Nordisk. Then, after a buyout in 1995, Ms. Marrone founded AgraQuest, a natural pest management products company. She served as its CEO, chairman, and president until April 2006.

Today, at Marrone Organic Innovations, she leads a company whose goal is to make natural, effective, safe, and environmentally friendly pest management products.

Ms. Marrone serves on the boards of the Association of Applied IPM Ecologists, the National Foundation for IPM Education, and the Organic Farming Research Foundation. Since 1999 she has served on the board of Sutter Health's Sacramento-Sierra Region.

Sir Gerry Robinson is the former chairman of Allied Domecq, an international company that operated spirits and wine companies and quick-service restaurants.

After leaving college at age seventeen, Sir Gerry Robinson had planned to become a priest. Instead, in 1965, he joined Matchbox Toys, a company he stayed with for nine years before moving to Lex Service Group.

In 1980 he joined Grand Metropolitan as the Finance Director of the U.K. Coca-Cola business. He became managing director in 1982, then took up the mantle of chief executive of Grand Met's Contract Services Division. In 1987 he led the management buyout of the business from Grand Metropolitan.

He joined Granada as chief executive in 1991, latterly overseeing the company's takeover of Forte

About the Contributors

Hotels in 1996. He was then instrumental in the merger between Granada Group and Compass Group in 2000. He retired from Granada in 2001 and became chairman of Allied Domecq a year later. He stood down as chairman after a takeover by Pernod Ricard.

Currently Sir Gerry Robinson is chairman of Moto Hospitality Ltd., the United Kingdom's leading operator of motorway service areas.

Andrew Sherman is the cofounder and CEO of Grow Fast Grow Right, a world leader in the development and delivery of on-site and online executive and management training programs.

Mr. Sherman, a recognized corporate and transactional attorney, is also a partner in the Washington, D.C.–based law firm Dickstein Shapiro. He serves as a legal and strategic advisor to Fortune 500 and emerging growth companies.

Mr. Sherman has also served as an adjunct professor in the MBA programs at the University of Maryland for more than eighteen years. Since 1987 he has been outside general counsel to the Young Entrepreneurs' Organization and he is chairman of the board/general counsel to the Small and Emerging Contractors Advisory Forum. He is the former chairman of the National Commission on Entrepreneurship.

Mike Southon is the chairman of Beermat Ecademy and the coauthor of *The Beermat Entrepreneur.*

About the Contributors

In 1994 Mr. Southon cofounded Instruction Set, a software consultancy, which he sold in 1989 and left in 1991.

From 1991 to 1995 he played in a band, and in 1995 he began helping entrepreneurs with their start-up companies. In 2002 Mr. Southon co-authored *The Beermat Entrepeneur*, one of the bestselling business books in the United Kingdom, and the first in a series of successful business books.

Among his recent customers are Accenture, Goldman Sachs, GlaxoSmithKline, Rolls-Royce, and the Royal Bank of Scotland.

⊰ ACKNOWLEDGMENTS ⊱

First and foremost, a heartfelt thanks goes
to all of the entrepreneurs and executives
who have candidly shared their hard-earned
experience and battle-tested insights for the
Lessons Learned series.

The precise guidance and generous access
to executives provided by both Karen Kerri-
gan from the Small Business and Entrepreneurship Council and Kay Koplovitz and
Amy Millman from Springboard Enterprises
were indispensable to the success of this
book. We are grateful for their enthusiasm.

Angelia Herrin, at Harvard Business
School Publishing, consistently offered un-
wavering support, good humor, and counsel from the inception of this ambitious
project.

Brian Surrette, Hollis Heimbouch, and
David Goehring provided invaluable edito-
rial direction, perspective, and encourage-
ment. Much appreciation goes to Jennifer

Acknowledgments

Lynn for her research and diligent attention to detail. Many thanks to the entire HBSP team of designers, copy editors, and marketing professionals who helped bring this series to life.

Finally, thanks to our fellow cofounder James MacKinnon and the entire Fifty Lessons team for the tremendous amount of time, effort, and steadfast support for this project.

—Adam Sodowick
   Andy Hasoon
   Directors and Cofounders
   Fifty Lessons

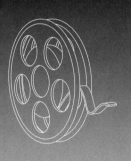